BLAZERS

— BUILDING A —

MOTORCYCLE

BY TYLER OMOTH

CONTENT CONSULTANT
WADE BARTLETT, PE,
MECHANICAL FORENSICS
ENGINEERING SERVICES, LLC
ROCHESTER, NEW HAMPSHIRE

READING CONSULTANT
BARBARA J. FOX
PROFESSOR EMERITA
NORTH CAROLINA STATE UNIVERSITY

CAPSTONE PRESS
a capstone imprint

Blazers Books are published by Capstone Press,
1710 Roe Crest Drive, North Mankato, Minnesota 56003
www.capstonepub.com

Library of Congress Cataloging-in-Publication Data
Omoth, Tyler.
  Building a motorcycle / by Tyler Omoth.
      pages cm — (Blazers. See how it's made.)
  Audience: Age 9.
  Audience: Grades 4 to 6.
  Summary: "Describes the process of building a motorcycle"—Provided by publisher.
  Includes bibliographical references and index.
  ISBN 978-1-4765-3977-5 (library binding)
  ISBN 978-1-4765-5117-3 (paperback)
  ISBN 978-1-4765-5958-2 (ebook pdf)
  1. Motorcycles—Design and construction—Juvenile literature. I. Title.
  TL440.15.O47 2014
  629.2'34—dc23   2013032490

Editorial Credits
Mandy Robbins, editor; Kyle Grenz, designer; Kathy McColley, production specialist

Photo Credits
Alamy: claude thibault, 29, imagebroker/Jacek Bilski, 12, 17, james cheadle, 25, ZUMA Press/
Minneapolis Star Tribune/Richard Sennott, 23; AP Images: Orlin Wagner, 14; Bloomberg via Getty
Images: Kuni Takahashi, 18; Corbis: Imaginechina, 8, Rick Friedman, 11; Newscom: SIPA/Durand
Florence, 20-21, 26-27; Shutterstock: Dmitry Zaltsman, 4, Gayvoronskaya_Yana, cover (background),
Harsanyi Andras, 1, Lario Tus, cover (motorcycle), Nikkolia, cover, 1 (inset laser), rook76, 7,
sparkdesign, throughout (background)

Printed in the United States of America in Stevens Point, Wisconsin.
092013   007768WZS14

TABLE OF CONTENTS

TWO WHEELS ON THE ROAD

Before a motorcycle cruises down the road, every wire, nut, and bolt must be in place. There are hundreds of parts in a motorcycle. See how these machines are built for highway driving or winding through forest trails.

MAIN MOTORCYCLE MANUFACTURERS AROUND THE WORLD

Manufacturer	Headquarters	Main types of motorcycles made
APRILIA	NOALE, ITALY	DIRT BIKES, SPORT BIKES
BMW	MUNICH, GERMANY	TOURING, SPORT BIKES
DUCATI	BOLOGNA, ITALY	SPORT BIKES
HARLEY-DAVIDSON	MILWAUKEE, WISCONSIN	CRUISERS, TOURING
HONDA	HAMAMATSU, JAPAN	CRUISERS, TOURING, DIRT BIKES, SPORT BIKES
TRIUMPH	HINCKLEY, ENGLAND	CRUISERS, SPORT BIKES
KTM	MATTIGHOFEN, AUSTRIA	DIRT BIKES, SPORT BIKES
YAMAHA	IWATA, JAPAN	CRUISERS, TOURING, DIRT BIKES, SPORT BIKES
KAWASAKI	AKASHI, JAPAN	CRUISERS, TOURING, DIRT BIKES, SPORT BIKES

TYPES OF MOTORCYCLES

cruiser—a style of street motorcycle that is middleweight and built to be comfortable for highway riding; the rider sits back with legs and arms forward

dirt bike—a style of motorcycle that is lightweight and rugged for riding off-road

sport bike—a style of motorcycle that is built for speed and performance; the rider generally leans forward

touring—a style of street motorcycle that is generally large, heavy, and built to be comfortable for long rides

FIRST STEPS

Before a motorcycle is built, designers plan each part, from the **frame** to the **throttle**. They make computer models to test different engines and body styles.

frame—the main body of a bike
throttle—a twist-grip on the right handlebar that controls the flow of fuel to the engine

FACT
Sylvester Roper built the
first motorcycle in 1867.
It was powered by steam.

MELTED STEEL

Metal, plastic, and rubber are the main materials used to make motorcycles. Some of these materials must be very strong. Others must be very flexible. Workers use machines that cut and mold materials to create the pieces needed to build the bike.

CHAPTER 2

BUILDING THE MOTORCYCLE

Most motorcycles are built in large factories with **assembly lines**. Each person or robot adds one piece to each motorcycle as it passes by. Making bikes this way lets **manufacturers** build many motorcycles quickly.

assembly line—a group of workers and machines that puts products together; products pass from one station to the next until the job is done
manufacturer—a company that makes products

FRAME

For most motorcycles, the metal frame is built first. It is welded to the right shape for each bike. The frame needs to be strong enough to handle the stress of riding. Bumps, speeding up, and slowing down all stress the frame.

FACT
The world's smallest working motorcycle was just 2.5 inches (6 centimeters) tall and 4.5 inches (11 cm) long. Tom Wiberg built it in 2003.

weld—to join two pieces of metal by heating them until they melt together

ENGINE

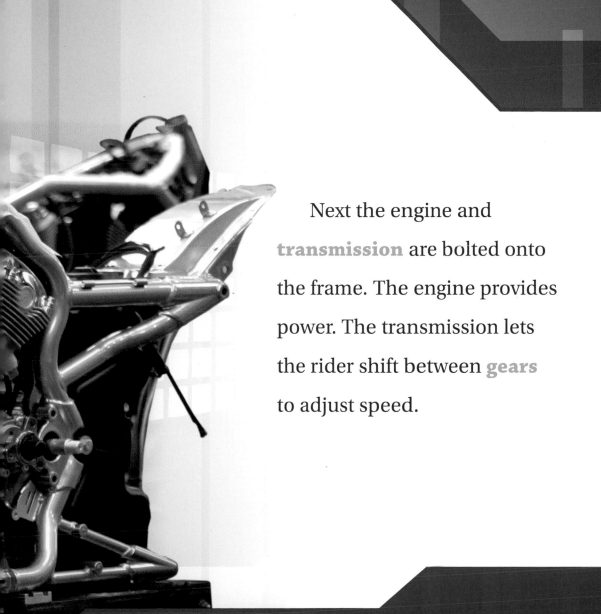

Next the engine and **transmission** are bolted onto the frame. The engine provides power. The transmission lets the rider shift between **gears** to adjust speed.

transmission—the series of gears in a vehicle that sends power from the engine to the wheels

gear—a toothed wheel that fits into another wheel; gears can change the direction of force or transfer power

An exhaust pipe is attached
to the engine. It allows gases to
flow away from the engine.
A muffler is put on the end to
lower noise.

exhaust—the waste gases produced by an engine

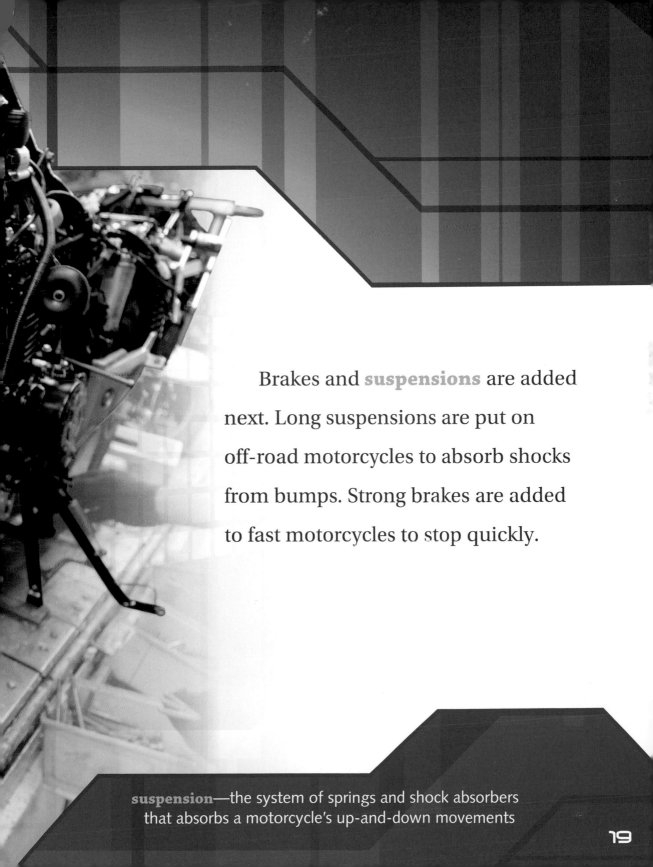

Brakes and **suspensions** are added next. Long suspensions are put on off-road motorcycles to absorb shocks from bumps. Strong brakes are added to fast motorcycles to stop quickly.

suspension—the system of springs and shock absorbers that absorbs a motorcycle's up-and-down movements

Next workers put on the tires. Different bikes need different tires. Street bikes have smooth tires for riding on pavement. Dirt bikes have knobby tires to help grip the dirt.

Molded metal or plastic create the **bodywork** of the motorcycle. Workers spray-paint some of the bodywork before it is attached to the frame. They use **chrome** on other parts.

FACT
The fastest motorcycles have bodywork that wraps all the way around the bike. This style glides through the air more easily.

bodywork—the outside shell of a motor vehicle
chrome—a coating that gives objects a shiny, metallic appearance

CHAPTER 3

FINISHING TOUCHES

Once the main parts are in place, workers add finishing touches. They fasten foot pegs, throttles, and shift levers to help control the bike. **Gauges** are added to inform riders about fuel, speed, and how the engine is running.

gauge—an instrument in a vehicle that shows how the vehicle is operating

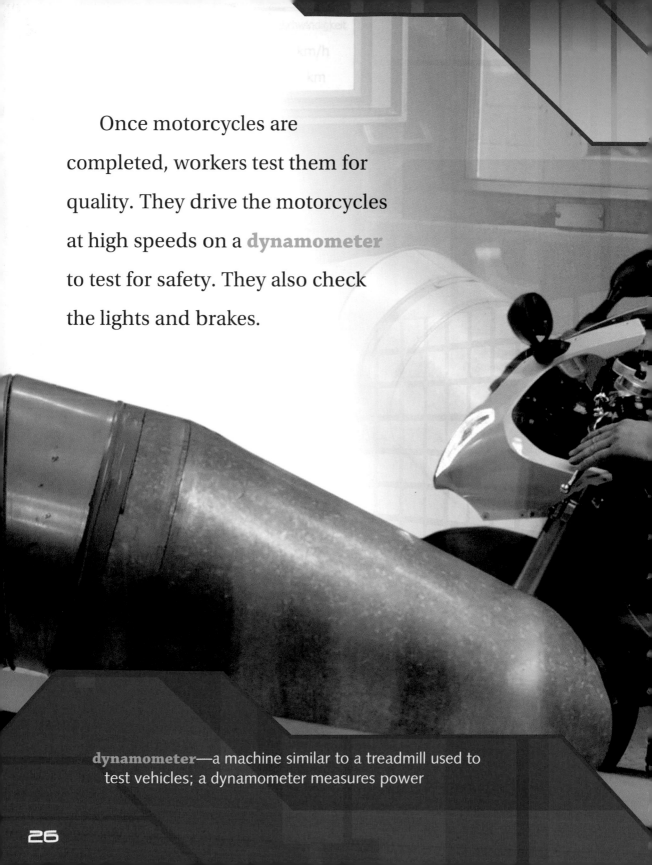

Once motorcycles are completed, workers test them for quality. They drive the motorcycles at high speeds on a **dynamometer** to test for safety. They also check the lights and brakes.

dynamometer—a machine similar to a treadmill used to test vehicles; a dynamometer measures power

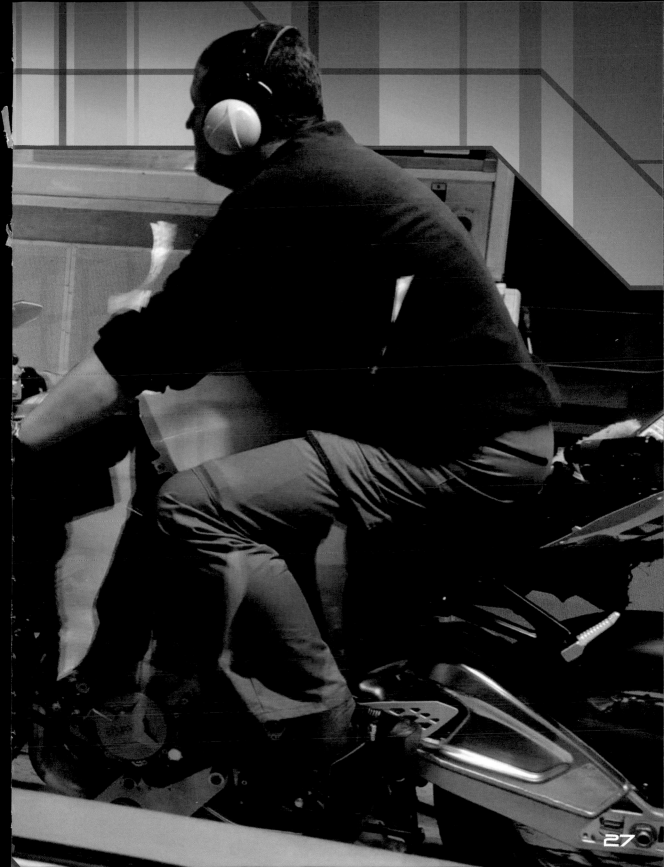

CHAPTER 4

READY FOR THE ROAD

The finished motorcycle is cleaned and polished to a high shine. It leaves the factory and is shipped to a showroom. The only step left is for someone to buy it and hit the open road!

FACT
Motorcycle riders gather at rallies to enjoy their bikes. In 2012 more than 400,000 people attended the motorcycle rally in Sturgis, South Dakota.

GLOSSARY

assembly line (uh-SEM-blee LYN)—a group of workers and machines that puts products together; products pass from one station to the next until the job is done

bodywork (BAH-dee-werk)—the outside shell of a motor vehicle

chrome (KROHM)—a coating that gives objects a shiny, metallic appearance

dynamometer (dy-nuh-MAH-mih-tuhr)—a machine similar to a treadmill used to test vehicles; a dynamometer measures power

exhaust (eg-ZAWST)—the waste gases produced by an engine

frame (FRAYM)—the main body of a bike

gauge (GAYJ)—an instrument in a vehicle that shows how the vehicle is operating

gear (GEER)—a toothed wheel that fits into another wheel; gears can change the direction of force or transfer power

manufacturer (man-yuh-FAK-chur-uhr)—a person or company that makes products

suspension (suh-SPEN-shuhn)—the system of springs and shock absorbers that absorbs a motorcycle's up-and-down movements

throttle (THROT-uhl)—a lever that controls the flow of fuel to the engine

transmission (trans-MISH-uhn)—the series of gears in a vehicle that sends power from the engine to the wheels

weld (WELD)—to join two pieces of metal by heating them until they melt together

READ MORE

Gillespie, Lisa Jane. *Motorcycles.* Tulsa, Okla.: Edc. Publishing, 2011.

Hill, Lee Sullivan. *Motorcycles on the Move.* Vroom-Vroom. Minneapolis: Lerner Publications Co., 2011.

Nixon, James. *Motorcycles.* Machines on the Move. Mankato, Minn.: Amicus, 2011.

INTERNET SITES

FactHound offers a safe, fun way to find Internet sites related to this book. All of the sites on FactHound have been researched by our staff.

Here's all you do:

Visit *www.facthound.com*

Type in this code: 9781476539775

INDEX